MEMORABLE STORIES AND PARABLES BY BOYD K. PACKER

MEMORABLE STORIES AND PARABLES BY BOYD K. PACKER

BOOKCRAFT

Salt Lake City, Utah

Only standard works, official statements, and other
publications written under assignment from the
First Presidency and the Council of the Twelve Apostles
are considered authorized publications by
The Church of Jesus Christ of Latter-day Saints.
Other publications, including this one,
are the responsibility of the writer.

The Author

Library of Congress Catalog Card Number: 97-74251
ISBN 1-57008-336-3

First Printing, 1997

Printed in the United States of America

CONTENTS

1   A Still, Small Voice   *1*

2   Bringing in the Lost   *4*

3   The Mediator   *7*

4   Home Teacher Is Taught   *11*

5   The Balm of Gilead   *14*

6   Relief Society—a Refuge, a Type   *20*

7   Redeeming the Lost Sheep   *24*

8   High Standards Attract   *31*

9   The Only True and Living Church   *34*

10   Great Responsibility Rests on Teachers   *38*

11   Prayers and Answers   *42*

12   Give to the Needy   *45*

13   Keeping Covenants   *48*

14   Of Cars and Dates   *52*

15   Testimony Comes from Personal Revelation   *57*

16   Man's Dual Nature   *60*

17   Beware of Covenant Breakers   *62*

18   "Feed My Sheep"   *66*

19   Stay in Context   *73*

20   Forgiving Oneself   *77*

21   Channeling and Controlling Your Thoughts   *78*

22   Spiritual Crocodiles   *82*

23   Someone to Do For   *87*

24   What Do You Put Into It?   *88*

25   Premortal Life   *91*

26   The Inheritance—a Parable   *95*

Index   *99*

1

A STILL, SMALL VOICE

In the early days of their marriage my father and mother lived on a little farm at Corinne. It was very difficult to raise crops, so they were very poor.

One morning, my father had to go into town. He had broken a piece of farm equipment and it had to be welded before he could continue planting. He came to the house and told Mother he must go to the blacksmith in Brigham City, a distance of seven miles. Although Mother was in the middle of doing the weekly washing, she quickly made arrangements to go with him, for it was not often that she could go to town.

On the cook stove in the kitchen she had been heating water for the washing. She also had a kettle of water heating on top of a little stove in the bedroom. While she set her washing things aside, banked the fires, and quickly got the little children ready for the trip to town, she thought of all the things she could do while Father was at the blacksmith's.

In the meantime Father harnessed the horse and brought the buggy to the front gate. Mother hurried out with the children and lifted them into the buggy. As she began to climb into the buggy herself, she hesitated a moment and then said, "I think I won't go with you today."

"What's the matter?" Father asked.

"I don't know," she answered. "I just have the *feeling* that I shouldn't go."

When she said *feeling,* that meant something to my father. He was wise enough not to tease her or try to talk her out of it. He simply said, "Well, if you have that feeling, perhaps you had better stay home."

As she lifted the children out of the buggy, you can imagine what they did!

She watched Father as the buggy went down the road then clattered across the bridge over the Bear River, up the bank on the opposite side, and out of sight. She stood at the gate with the children, who were crying in disappointment, and said to herself, "Now, wasn't that silly of me?"

She returned to the little house with the thought of finishing the washing.

I should tell you that that was a very humble home. The ceiling was not wood or plaster, but was made of cloth stretched and sized with glue and then wallpapered. They did that in homes in those days—not in the expensive homes but in the very humble homes.

The chimney pipe of the little stove in the bedroom was insulated with a brass ring at the point where it went through the fabric ceiling. No one knew that above the ceiling the pipe had rusted through. Now, sparks had escaped into the attic and settled into the dust. Mother had been back in the home only a few minutes when she smelled smoke and found the ceiling afire.

The little youngsters formed a bucket brigade from the pump. Mother stood on a chair and threw the water to the ceiling, and soon the fire was out.

And so the incident closes, except to ask the very important question: Why didn't she go to town that day?

Father and Mother had prayed earnestly that the Lord would bless them to be able to raise their family—feed them, clothe them, and provide shelter for them. They had been saving money to pay for their farm, and their savings were hidden away in that little house. All they owned was somehow centered in that humble home. To lose it would have been a great tragedy.

This little Danish mother of mine had prayed many times that they might be blessed. On that day her prayers were dramatically answered.

Again the question: Why did she not go to town that day?

She did not hear an audible voice saying, "Emma, you'd better not go to town today, I'm going to answer your prayers." Nor did a written message descend from which she could read, "Emma, you'd better stay home today." She stayed home because of a feeling; a still, small voice had spoken to her. She told my father, "I just have the *feeling* that I shouldn't go."

It was a great lesson my little Danish mother taught us.

2

BRINGING IN THE LOST

As a reminder to the Church members of our obligation to share the gospel I repeat an account from the history of the Church.

In the late 1850s many converts from Europe were struggling to reach the Great Salt Lake Valley. Many were too poor to afford the open and the covered wagons and had to walk, pulling their meager belongings in handcarts. Some of the most touching and tragic moments in the history of the Church accompanied these handcart pioneers.

One such company was commanded by a Brother McArthur. Archer Walters, an English convert who was with the company, recorded in his diary under 2 July 1856 this sentence: "Brother Parker's little boy, age six, was lost, and the father went back to hunt him."

The boy, Arthur, was next to the youngest of the four children of Robert and Ann Parker. Three days earlier the company had hurriedly made camp in the face of a sudden thunderstorm. It was then that the boy was missed. The parents had thought him to be playing along the way with the other children.

Someone remembered that earlier in the day, when they had stopped, he had seen the little boy settle down to rest under the shade of some brush.

Now, most of you have little children and you know how quickly a tired little six-year-old could fall asleep on a sultry summer day and how soundly he could sleep, so that even the noise of the camp moving on might not waken him.

For two days the company remained, and all of the men searched for him. Then on July 2, with no alternative, the company was ordered west.

Robert Parker, as the diary records, went back alone to search once more for his little son. As he was leaving camp, his wife pinned a bright shawl about his shoulders with words such as these: "If you find him dead, wrap him in the shawl to bury him. If you find him alive, you could use this as a flag to signal us."

She, with the other little children, took the handcart and struggled along with the company.

Out on the trail each night Ann Parker kept watch. At sundown on July 5, as they were watching, they saw a figure approaching from the east! Then in the rays of the setting sun she saw the glimmer of the bright red shawl.

One of the diaries records: "Ann Parker fell in a pitiful heap upon the sand, and that night, for the first time in six nights she slept."

Under July 5, Brother Walters recorded: "Brother Parker brings into camp his little boy that had been lost. Great joy through the camp. The mother's joy I can not describe." (LeRoy R. Hafen and Ann W. Hafen, *Handcarts to Zion* [Glendale, California: The Arthur H. Clark Co., 1960], p. 61.)

We do not know all of the details. A nameless woods-man—I've often wondered how unlikely it was that a woodsman should be there—found the little boy and described him as being sick with illness and with terror, and he cared for him until his father found him.

So here a story, commonplace in its day, ends—except for a question. In Ann Parker's place, how would you feel toward the nameless woodsman who had saved your little son? Would there be any end to your gratitude?

To sense this is to feel something of the gratitude our Father must feel toward any of us who saves one of his children. Such gratitude is a prize dearly to be won, for the Lord has said, "If it so be that you should labor all your days in crying repentance unto this people, and bring, save it be one soul unto me, how great shall be your joy with him in the kingdom of my Father?" (D&C 18:15.) Even so, I might add, if that soul should be our own.

3

THE MEDIATOR

There once was a man who wanted something very much. It seemed more important than anything else in his life. In order for him to have his desire, he incurred a great debt.

He had been warned about going into that much debt, and particularly about his creditor. But it seemed so important for him to do what he wanted to do and to have what he wanted right now. He was sure he could pay for it later.

So he signed a contract. He would pay if off sometime along the way. He didn't worry too much about it, for the due date seemed such a long time away. He had what he wanted now, and that was what seemed important.

The creditor was always somewhere in the back of his mind, and he made token payments now and again, thinking somehow that the day of reckoning really would never come.

But as it always does, the day came, and the contract fell due. The debt had not been fully paid. His creditor appeared and demanded payment in full.

Only then did he realize that his creditor not only had the power to repossess all that he owned, but the power to cast him into prison as well.

"I cannot pay you, for I have not the power to do so," he confessed.

"Then," said the creditor, "we will exercise the contract, take your possessions, and you shall go to prison. You agreed to that. It was your choice. You signed the contract, and now it must be enforced."

"Can you not extend the time or forgive the debt?" the debtor begged. "Arrange some way for me to keep what I have and not go to prison. Surely you believe in mercy? Will you not show mercy?"

The creditor replied, "Mercy is always so one-sided. It would serve only you. If I show mercy to you, it will leave me unpaid. It is justice I demand. Do you believe in justice?"

"I believed in justice when I signed the contract," the debtor said. "It was on my side then, for I thought it would protect me. I did not need mercy then, nor think I should need it ever. Justice, I thought, would serve both of us equally as well."

"It is justice that demands that you pay the contract or suffer the penalty," the creditor replied. "That is the law. You have agreed to it and that is the way it must be. Mercy cannot rob justice."

There they were: One meting out justice, the other pleading for mercy. Neither could prevail except at the expense of the other.

"If you do not forgive the debt there will be no mercy," the debtor pleaded.

"If I do, there will be no justice," was the reply.

Both laws, it seemed, could not be served. They are two eternal ideals that appear to contradict one another. Is there no way for justice to be fully served, and mercy also?

There is a way! The law of justice *can* be fully satisfied and mercy *can* be fully extended—but it takes someone else. And so it happened this time.

The debtor had a friend. He came to help. He knew the debtor well. He knew him to be shortsighted. He thought him foolish to have gotten himself into such a predicament. Nevertheless, he wanted to help because he loved him. He stepped between them, faced the creditor, and made this offer.

"I will pay the debt if you will free the debtor from his contract so that he may keep his possessions and not go to prison."

As the creditor was pondering the offer, the mediator added, "You demanded justice. Though he cannot pay you, I will do so. You will have been justly dealt with and can ask no more. It would not be just."

And so the creditor agreed.

The mediator turned then to the debtor. "If I pay your debt, will you accept me as your creditor?"

"Oh yes, yes," cried the debtor. "You save me from prison and show mercy to me."

"Then," said the benefactor, "you will pay the debt to

me and I will set the terms. It will not be easy, but it will be possible. I will provide a way. You need not go to prison."

And so it was that the creditor was paid in full. He had been justly dealt with. No contract had been broken.

The debtor, in turn, had been extended mercy. Both laws stood fulfilled. Because there was a mediator, justice had claimed its full share, and mercy was fully satisfied.

Each of us lives on a kind of spiritual credit. One day the account will be closed, a settlement demanded. However casually we may view it now, when that day comes and the foreclosure is imminent we will look around in restless agony for someone, anyone, to help us.

And, by eternal law, mercy cannot be extended save there be one who is both willing and able to assume our debt and pay the price and arrange the terms for our redemption.

Unless there is a mediator, unless we have a friend, the full weight of justice untempered, unsympathetic, must, positively must, fall on us. The full recompense for every transgression, however minor or however deep, will be exacted from us to the uttermost farthing.

But know this: Truth, glorious truth, proclaims there is such a mediator.

"For there is one God, and one mediator between God and men, the man Christ Jesus" (1 Timothy 2:5).

Through Him mercy can be fully extended to each of us without offending the eternal law of justice.

4

HOME TEACHER IS TAUGHT

In my experience I recall a very significant lesson I learned as a home teacher.

Shortly before I was married I was assigned with an older companion to serve as home teacher to an aged little lady who was a shut-in. She was a semi-invalid, and often when we knocked on the door she would call us to come in. We would find her unable to be about and would leave our message at her bedside.

We somehow learned that she was very partial to lemon ice cream. Frequently we would stop at the ice cream store before making our visit. Because we knew her favorite flavor, there were two reasons why we were welcome into that home.

On one occasion the senior companion was not able to go, for reasons that I do not remember, so I went alone. I followed the ritual of getting a half-pint of lemon ice cream before making the call.

I found the old lady in bed. She expressed a great worry over a grandchild who was to undergo a very serious operation the following day. She asked if I would kneel at the side of her bed and offer a prayer for the well-being of the youngster.

After the prayer—thinking, I suppose, of my coming marriage—she said, "Tonight I will teach you." She said she wanted to tell me something and that I was always to remember it. Then began the lesson I have never forgotten. She recounted something of her life.

A few years after her marriage to a fine young man in the temple, when they were concentrating on the activities of young married life and raising a young family, one day a letter came from "Box B." (In those days a letter from Box B in Salt Lake City was invariably a mission call.)

To their surprise they were called as a family to go to one of the far continents of the world to help open the land for missionary work. They served faithfully and well, and after several years they returned to their home to set about again the responsibilities of raising their family.

Then this little woman focused in on a Monday morning. It could perhaps be called a blue washday Monday. There had been some irritation and a disagreement; then some biting words between husband and wife. Interestingly enough, she couldn't remember how it all started or what it was over. "But," she said, "nothing would do but that I follow him to the gate, and as he walked up the street on his way to work I just had to call that last biting, spiteful remark after him."

Then, as the tears began to flow, she told me of an accident that took place that day, as a result of which he never returned. "For fifty years," she sobbed, "I've lived in hell knowing that the last words he heard from my lips were that biting, spiteful remark."

This was the message to her young home teacher. She pressed it upon me with the responsibility never to forget it. I have profited greatly from it. I have come to know since that time that a couple can live together without one cross word ever passing between them.

I have often wondered about those visits to that home, about the time I spent and the few cents we spent on ice cream. That little sister is long since gone beyond the veil. This is true also of my senior companion. But the powerful experience of that home teaching, the home teacher being taught, is with me yet, and I have found occasion to leave her message with young couples at the marriage altar and in counseling people across the world.

*M*arriage is yet safe, with all its sweet fulfillment, with all its joy and love. In marriage all of the worthy yearnings of the human soul, all that is physical and emotional and spiritual, can be fulfilled.

5

THE BALM OF GILEAD

The Bible records that in ancient times there came from Gilead beyond the Jordan a substance used to heal and soothe. It came, perhaps, from a tree or shrub and was a major commodity of trade in the ancient world. It was known as the Balm of Gilead. That name became symbolic for the power to soothe and heal. . . .

All of us experience some temporary physical sickness. All of us now and again may be spiritually ill as well. Too many of us, however, are chronically spiritually sick.

We don't need to stay that way. We can learn to avoid spiritual infections and maintain good spiritual health. Even though we have a serious physical ailment, we can be spiritually healthy.

If you suffer from worry, from grief or shame, from jealousy, disappointment, or envy, I have something to tell you.

Somewhere near your home there is a vacant corner lot. Although adjoining yards may be well tended, a vacant corner lot somehow is always full of weeds.

There is a footpath across it, a bicycle trail, and ordinarily it is a collecting place for junk. First someone threw a few lawn clippings there. They would not hurt anything. Someone added a few sticks and limbs from a nearby yard. Then came a few papers and a plastic bag, and finally some tin cans and old bottles were included.

And there it was—a junkyard. . . .

This corner lot is like, so very much like, the minds of many of us. We leave our minds vacant and empty and open to trespass by anyone. Whatever is dumped there we keep. . . .

I do not want anything coming into my mind that does not have some useful purpose or some value that makes it worth keeping. I have enough trouble keeping the weeds down that sprout there on their own without permitting someone else to clutter my mind with things that do not edify. . . .

I've had to evict some thoughts a hundred times before they would stay out. I have never been successful until I have put something edifying in their place.

I do not want my mind to be a dumping place for shabby ideas or thoughts, for disappointments, bitterness, envy, shame, hatred, worry, grief, or jealousy.

If you are fretting over such things, it's time to clean the yard. Get rid of all that junk! Get rid of it! . . .

Many years ago I was taught a lesson by a man I admired very much. He was as saintly a man as I have ever known. He was steady and serene, with a deep spiritual strength that many drew upon. . . .

On one occasion when we were alone and the spirit was

right, he gave me a lesson for my life from an experience in his. Although I thought I had known him, he told me things I would not have supposed.

He grew up in a little community. Somehow in his youth he had a desire to make something of himself and struggled successfully to get an education. He married a lovely young woman and presently everything in his life was just right. He was well employed with a bright future. They were deeply in love and she was expecting their first child.

The night the baby was to be born there were complications. The only doctor was somewhere in the countryside tending to the sick. They were not able to find him. After many hours of labor the condition of the mother-to-be became desperate.

Finally the doctor arrived. He sensed the emergency, acted quickly, and soon had things in order. The baby was born and the crisis, it appeared, was over.

Some days later the young mother died from the very infection that the doctor had been treating at the other home that night.

My friend's world was shattered. Everything was not right now; everything was all wrong. He had lost his wife, his sweetheart. He had no way to take care of a tiny baby and at once tend to his work.

As the weeks wore on his grief festered. "That doctor should not be allowed to practice," he would say. "He brought that infection to my wife; if he had been careful she would be alive today." He thought of little else, and in his bitterness he became threatening.

Then one night a knock came at his door. A little youngster said, simply: "Daddy wants you to come over. He wants to talk to you."

"Daddy" was the stake president. A grieving, heartbroken young man went to see his spiritual leader. This spiritual shepherd had been watching his flock and had something to say to him.

The counsel from this wise servant was simply: "John, leave it alone. Nothing you do about it will bring her back. Anything you do will make it worse. John, leave it alone."

My friend told me then that this had been his trial, his Gethsemane.

How could he leave it alone? Right was right! A terrible wrong had been committed, and somebody must pay for it.

He struggled in agony to get hold of himself. It did not happen at once. Finally he determined that whatever else the issues were, he should be obedient.

Obedience is a powerful spiritual medicine. It comes close to being a cure-all.

He determined to follow the counsel of that wise spiritual leader. He would leave it alone.

Then he told me: "I was an old man before I finally understood. It was not until I was an old man that I could finally see a poor country doctor—overworked, underpaid, run ragged from patient to patient, with little proper medicine, no hospital, few instruments. He struggled to save lives, and succeeded for the most part.

"He had come in a moment of crisis when two lives hung in the balance and had acted without delay.

"I was an old man," he repeated, "before finally I understood. I would have ruined my life," he said, "and the lives of others."

Many times he had thanked the Lord on his knees for a wise spiritual leader who counseled simply, "John, leave it alone."

And that is my counsel to you. If you have festering sores, a grudge, some bitterness, disappointment, or jealousy, get hold of yourself. You may not be able to control things out there with others, but you can control things here, inside of you.

I say, therefore: John, leave it alone. Mary, leave it alone.

You may need a transfusion of spiritual strength to be able to do this. Then just ask for it. We call that prayer. Prayer is powerful, spiritual medicine. The instructions for its use are found in the scriptures.

One of our sacred hymns carries this message:

> *Ere you left your room this morning,*
> *Did you think to pray? . . .*
> *When your soul was full of sorrow,*
> *Balm of Gilead did you borrow*
> *At the gates of day?*
> *Oh, how praying rests the weary!*
> *Prayer will change the night to day.*
> *So, when life gets dark and dreary,*
> *Don't forget to pray.*

All of us carry excess baggage around from time to time, but the wisest ones among us don't carry if for very long. They get rid of it. . . .

[The Savior] has said: "Peace I leave with you, my peace I give unto you: not as the world giveth, give I unto you. Let not your heart be troubled, neither let it be afraid." (John 14:27.)

If you, my brother or sister, are troubled, there is at hand, not just in Gilead, a soothing, healing balm.

6

RELIEF SOCIETY—
A REFUGE, A TYPE

The Relief Society might be likened to a refuge—the place of safety and protection, the sanctuary of ancient times. You will be safe within it. It encircles each sister like a protecting wall.

We turn to the Old Testament for a lesson. When the Israelites returned from their long captivity in Babylon, they found their city in ruins. The protecting walls of Jerusalem lay in rubble. Their enemies moved among them with great influence, and the Israelites were subject to them.

Then came Nehemiah the prophet, known now as "the wall builder." He rallied the Israelites to their own defense. Under his direction they began to rebuild the wall.

At first their enemies ridiculed them. Tobiah, the Ammonite, mocked them, saying, "Even that which they build, if a fox go up, he shall even break down their stone wall" (Nehemiah 4:3).

But Nehemiah consoled his people and set to work. The enemy was everywhere. "Nevertheless," he recorded, "we made [a] prayer unto our God, and set a watch against them" (Nehemiah 4:9).

Sisters, think carefully upon that. They "made a prayer," and "set a watch," and proceeded with their work.

The day came when their enemies saw that the wall was completed. It encircled the city. No breach was left, save it were the place for the gates. What their enemies had ridiculed was nearly done. The wall now stood. No longer could their enemies threaten nor destroy. When their enemies saw that the Israelites grew strong, they worried, and they turned to other tactics.

And here is the lesson. It is a type, it is symbolic, it is a warning! In it is a message for every sister in Relief Society; for the general presidency and their board; for the stake and ward officers and teachers; indeed, for every member. Consider it very, very carefully.

Sanballat and Tobiah and Geshem sent for Nehemiah. "Come," they enticed, "let us meet together in some one of the villages in the plain of Ono." They endeavored to draw him away from his work on the wall. But the prophet knew their hearts and said, "They thought to do me mischief." (Nehemiah 6:2.)

Five times they sent for him to come out to them. Their importuning came then, just as it comes now to us: "Come parley with us, come join our cause, come do things our way. Come out into the world and be part with us."

His answer to them holds counsel for every sister in

Relief Society. It is a message as well to the brethren of the priesthood. "I sent messengers unto them," Nehemiah recorded, "saying, I am doing a great work, so that I cannot come down: why should the work cease, whilst I leave it, and come down to you?" (Nehemiah 6:3.)

Sisters, you have a great work to do. Build Relief Society! Strengthen its organization! Do not be enticed to leave it and go down to the worldly plains of Ono.

Do not allow yourselves to be organized under another banner. Do not run to and fro seeking some cause to fulfill your needs. Your cause stands under the authority of the priesthood of Almighty God; that is the consummate, the ultimate, power extant upon this earth! . . .

Oh, how powerful the tender, tempering teachings and the disarming wisdom of our sisters can be. I found the spirit of Relief Society—the whole of it—in the quiet reply of one sister.

Someone ridiculed her determination to gather her year's supply. She had stored enough for herself and her husband, with some to spare for her young married children who were without the means or the space to provide much for themselves. She told him she did it because the prophets had counseled us to do it. He chided her: "In the crunch you won't have it anyway. What if your leaders call everything in? You'd have to share it with those who didn't prepare. What will you think then?"

"If that should happen," she said, "at least I will have something to bring."

God bless you sisters of the Relief Society who bring so much.

In the Church we are not neutral. We are one-sided.
There is a war going on, and we are engaged in it.
It is the war between good and evil,
and we are belligerents defending the good.
We are therefore obliged to give preference to and
protect all that is represented in the gospel of Jesus Christ,
and we have made covenants to do it.

7

REDEEMING THE LOST SHEEP

The *Deseret News* of 10 July 1956 printed a bulletin from
the LDS Hospital on the condition of an eighteen-year-old
girl who had been brought to the hospital six days earlier
having survived nine days pinned under a car in Parley's
Canyon, near Salt Lake City. The bulletin was, for a change,
optimistic: "Attending physicians at the LDS Hospital said
the girl's blood condition is so improved she likely will need
no more transfusions. . . . Doctors said her diet has been in-
creased to include potatoes, eggs, and puddings. She no
longer requires intravenous feedings."

The injuries she had sustained in the accident were not
of themselves the important factor. It was the lack of food
and moisture that reduced her body to that poor condition.
It was several days before the doctors gave much hope for
her recovery.

It isn't easy to minister to one so starved. It was not a
matter of just putting food before her. The food had to be
carefully administered, for delicate balances could be upset,

and her life was at stake. Doctors were extremely careful, for their very treatment might prove fatal. When she recovered, that was regarded as something of a miracle.

So it is with those around us who are spiritually undernourished, or starved. We refer to them as the lost sheep. We are called to minister to them. They are of all descriptions. Some have deficiencies of one kind or another that merely rob them of spiritual vigor. Others have so seriously starved themselves of spiritual things that we scarce can hope to save them.

Responsibility for redemption of the lost sheep rests with the priesthood. The doing of it rests upon the home teacher. . . .

What can improve our ability, as individuals or as organizations, to redeem the lost sheep? What "vitamin" sparks an appetite for spiritual things?

In the April 1964 issue of the *Improvement Era* there appeared an article by Wilford B. Lee entitled "John Is Inactive . . . Why?" The author pointed out that knowledge does not necessarily control activity. Thus many know what they ought to do but fail to do it, even after encouragement from home teachers.

As regards righteous behavior, then, to know intellectually is not enough. The *feelings* must be engaged. . . . Alma recognized what would redeem the lost sheep. He knew what the moving power was. He saw "no way that he might reclaim them save it were in bearing down in pure testimony against them" (Alma 4:19).

Testimony, then, is the moving power. Testimony is the redeeming force. . . .

If you who hold positions in the Church would redeem the lost sheep, see that the "vitamins" go to those with deficiencies and not merely to those who are nourished by regular, balanced diets. . . .

At a ward sacrament meeting I attended recently a sister had been invited to sing whose husband was not active in the Church. He was, however, at the meeting. The bishop wanted a very special program for this occasion. His first announcement was: "Brother X, my first counselor, will give the opening prayer." His second counselor gave the closing prayer.

How unfortunate, I thought. The three men in the bishopric struggle with such concern over the spiritually sick, then take the very medicine that would make those people well—activity, participation—and consume it themselves in front of the needy! . . .

Several years ago I visited a stake presided over by a man of unusual efficiency and ability. Every detail of the stake conference had been scheduled. He had done the usual thing in assigning prayers from the selected circle of the stake presidency, the high council, the bishops, and the stake patriarch. Those brethren had not been notified, so we changed the assignment from those who deserved the honor to those who needed—desperately needed—the experience.

The president had a detailed agenda for the general sessions, and he mentioned that there were twenty minutes in one session that were not scheduled. I told him that we could call on some to respond who otherwise would not have the opportunity and needed the strengthening experience. He countered with the suggestion that he alert several able, prominent leaders to prepare for possible speaking assignments. "There will be many nonmembers present," he said. "We are used to having an organized and very polished conference performance. We have very able people in the stake. They will leave an excellent impression."

Twice again during our meeting he mentioned the schedule and pressed to have the stake's "best performers" called. "Why don't we save this time for those who need it most?" I said. His reaction was a disappointed, "Well, you are the General Authority."

Early Sunday morning he reminded me that there was still time to alert someone and thus leave the best impression.

The morning session was opened by the president with a polished and stirring address. Next we called on his second counselor. He was obviously flustered, and he began, "You can't believe a thing Brother Packer says." (We had previously indicated that both counselors would probably speak in the afternoon session.) We were to go to his home for the noon meal. He had known there would be time to go over his notes, so he had left them at home.

For want of his notes he turned to testimony, giving an inspiring account of an administration he had performed during the week. A brother, given up by his doctors, had been called from the very shadows of death by the power of the priesthood. I do not know what was on his notes, but surely it could not have compared in inspiration to the testimony he bore.

An elderly woman sat on the front row holding hands with a weathered-looking man. She looked a bit out of place in the fashionably dressed congregation—rather homespun by comparison. She looked as if she ought to talk in conference, and given the privilege she reported her mission. Fifty-two years before she had returned from the mission field, and since then she had never been invited to speak in church. It was a touching and moving witness that she bore.

Others were called upon to speak, and near the close of the meeting the president suggested that I take the remainder of the time. "Have you had any inspiration?" I asked. He said that he kept thinking of the mayor. (The voters in that large city had elected a member of the Church to be mayor, and he was in attendance.) When I told him we could have a greeting from the mayor, he whispered that the man was not active in the Church. When I suggested that he call upon him anyway he resisted, saying flatly that he was not worthy to speak in that meeting. At my insistence, however, he called the man to the stand.

The mayor's father had been a pioneer of the Church in that region. He had served as bishop of one of the wards and had been succeeded by one of his sons—a twin to the mayor, as I recall. The mayor was the lost sheep. He came to the pulpit and spoke, to my surprise, with bitterness and with hostility. His talk began something like this: "I don't know why you called on me. I don't know why I am in church today. I don't belong in church. I have never fit in. I don't agree with the way the Church does things."

I confess that I began to worry, but he then paused and lowered his eyes to the pulpit. From then until his talk was over he did not look up. After hesitating, he continued: "I guess I just as well tell you. I quit smoking six weeks ago." Then, shaking his fist in a gesture over his head towards the congregation, he said, "If any of you think that's easy, you have never suffered the hell I have suffered in the last few weeks."

Then he just melted. "I know the gospel is true," he said. "I've always known it was true. I learned that from my mother as a boy.

"I know the Church isn't out of order," he confessed. "It's me that's out of order, and I've always known that, too."

Then he spoke, perhaps, for all of the lost sheep when he pleaded: "I know it's me that is wrong, and I want to come back. I have been trying to come back, but you won't let me!"

Of course we would let him come back, but somehow we hadn't let him know that. After the meeting the congregation flooded up—not to us but to him, to say, "Welcome home!"

On the way to the airport after conference the stake president said to me, "I've learned a lesson today."

Hoping to confirm it, I said, "If we had done what you wanted to do you would have called on this man's father, wouldn't you, or perhaps his brother, the bishop?"

He nodded in affirmation and said: "Either of them, given five minutes, would have presented a stirring fifteen- or twenty-minute sermon to the approval of all in attendance. But no lost sheep would have been reclaimed."

All of us who lead in the wards and stakes must open the door to the lost sheep; stand aside to let them through. We must learn not to block the entrance. It is a narrow way. . . .

I do not appeal for the lowering of standards. Just the opposite. More lost sheep will respond quicker to high standards than they will to low ones. There is therapeutic value in spiritual discipline. . . .

Spiritual discipline framed in love and confirmed with testimony will help redeem souls.

---

*I readily confess that I would find no peace,
neither happiness nor safety, in a world without repentance.
I do not know what I should do if there were
no way for me to erase my mistakes.
The agony would be more than I could bear.*

8

HIGH STANDARDS ATTRACT

Several years ago I presided over one of our missions. Two of our missionaries were teaching a fine family who had expressed a desire to be baptized; and then they suddenly cooled off. The father had learned about tithing and he canceled all further meetings with the missionaries.

Two sad elders reported to the branch president, who himself was a recent convert, that he would not have this fine family in his branch.

A few days later the branch president persuaded the elders to join him in another visit to the family. "I understand," he told the father, "that you have decided not to join the Church."

"That is correct," the father answered.

"The elders tell me that you are disturbed about tithing."

"Yes," said the father. "They had not told us about it; and when I learned of it, I said, 'Now, that's too much to ask.' Our church has never asked anything like that. We think that's just too much and we will not join."

"Did they tell you about fast offering?" the president asked.

"No," said the man. "What is that?"

"In the Church we fast for two meals each month and give the value of the meals for the help of the poor."

"They did not tell us that," the man said.

"Did they mention the building fund?"

"No, what is that?"

"In the Church we all contribute toward building chapels. If you joined the Church, you would want to participate both in labor and with money. Incidentally, we are building a new chapel here," he told him.

"Strange," he said, "that they didn't mention it."

"Did they explain the welfare program to you?"

"No," said the father. "What is that?"

"Well, we believe in helping one another. If someone is in need or ill or out of work or in trouble, we are organized to assist, and you would be expected to help.

"Did they also tell you that we have no professional clergy? All of us contribute our time, our talents, our means, and travel—all to help the work. And we're not paid for it in money."

"They didn't tell us any of that," said the father.

"Well," said the branch president, "if you are turned away by a little thing like tithing, it is obvious you're not ready for this Church. Perhaps you have made the right decision and you should not join."

As they departed, almost as an afterthought he turned and said: "Have you ever wondered why people will do all of these things willingly? I have never received a bill for tithing. No one has ever called to collect it. But we pay it—and all of the rest—and count it as a great privilege.

"If you could discover *why*, you would be within reach of the pearl of great price, for which the Lord said the merchant man was willing to sell all that he had so that he might obtain it.

"But," the branch president added, "it is *your* decision. I only hope you will pray about it."

A few days later the man appeared at the branch president's home. No, he did not want to reschedule the missionaries. That would not be necessary. He wanted to schedule the baptism of his family. They had been praying, fervently praying.

This happens every day with individuals and entire families attracted by the high standards, not repelled by them.

9

THE ONLY TRUE AND
LIVING CHURCH

If there is a typical response to our missionaries, it is: "I already have a church. One is just as good as another and it doesn't matter really which one we belong to, or whether we belong to any. We will all end up in the same place anyway."

Surely no one who really thinks would hold to that position. Nevertheless many people accept it when they would not for a moment apply it or relate it to any other phase of their lives. They would not, for instance, take the same position with regard to education. Who would not smile at a statement that all schools are alike, that one is just as good as another, and that a person deserves the same diploma no matter which school he attends, or which course he takes, or for how long!

Would you agree to send students to just any school, taking any variety of courses, and then award them specialized degrees, anything they wanted—in architecture, law, medicine? Such an attitude would suggest that a man would be just as good a surgeon by not studying for it as he would be following the prerequisite courses. No person who has given it real, substantial thought would take such a position, and no one of us would want to be under the knife of a surgeon who had been trained, or maybe I should say untrained, in such a pattern.

Isn't it strange, then, that so many are able to apply such a view to religion? They advocate: Go to any school, take any course, or go to no school at all, and we'll all end up in the same place with the same heavenly diploma.

That just isn't reasonable, nor is it true.

The position that The Church of Jesus Christ of Latter-day Saints is the only true church upon the face of the earth is fundamental. Perhaps it would be more convenient and palatable and popular if we were to avoid this position; nevertheless we are under a sacred obligation and a sacred trust to hold to it. It is not merely an admission; it is a positive declaration. It is so fundamental that we cannot yield on this point. . . .

Now, this is not to say that the other churches, all of them, are totally without truth. They have some truth—some of them very much of it. They have a form of godliness. Often the clergy and the adherents are dedicated, and many of them practice well the virtues of Christianity. They are, nonetheless, incomplete. By the Lord's declaration, "they teach for doctrines the commandments of men, having a form of godliness, but they deny the power thereof" (Joseph Smith—History 1:19).

The gospel might be likened to the keyboard of a piano—a full keyboard with a selection of keys on which one who is trained can play a variety without limits: a ballad to express love, a march to rally, a sweet melody to soothe, and a hymn to inspire; an endless variety to suit every mood and satisfy every need.

How shortsighted it is, then, to choose a single key and endlessly tap out the monotony of a single note, or even two or three notes, when the full keyboard of limitless melody and harmony can be played!

How disappointing it is that when the fulness of the gospel, the whole keyboard, is here upon the earth, many churches tap on a single key! The note they stress may be essential to a complete harmony of religious experience, but nonetheless it is not all there is. It isn't the fulness.

For instance, one taps on the key of faith healing to the neglect of many principles that would bring greater strength than faith healing itself. Another taps on an obscure key relating to the observance of the Sabbath—a key that would sound different indeed if played in harmony with the other essential notes. A key used like that can get completely out of tune. Another repeats endlessly the key that relates to the mode of baptism and now and then taps one or two other keys as though there were not a full keyboard. And again, the very key used, essential as it is, just doesn't sound complete when played alone to the neglect of the others. . . .

We do not say the churches are wrong so much as we say they are incomplete. The fulness of the gospel has been restored. The power and the authority to act for God is present with us. The power and the authority of the priesthood rests upon this church. . . .

Now, the one-key danger is not limited to investigators. Some members of the Church who should know better pick out a hobby key or two and tap them incessantly, to the irritation of those around them. By doing this they can dull their own spiritual sensitivities. They can thus lose track of the inspired knowledge that there is a fulness of the gospel and can become, individually, as many churches have become: they may reject the fulness in preference to a favorite note. As this preference becomes exaggerated and distorted, they are led away into apostasy.

There is a sacred process by which pure intelligence may be conveyed into our minds and we can come to know instantly things that otherwise would take a long period of time to acquire. He can speak inspiration into our minds, especially when we are humble and seeking.

10

GREAT RESPONSIBILITY
RESTS ON TEACHERS

I reluctantly make reference to [an experience that] taught me a significant, fundamental lesson.

During the winter of 1943–44, World War II was raging in full intensity. I had enlisted in the United States Army Air Force, and after a number of months of preflight training was assigned to a primary training field near Scottsdale, Arizona. We were training in bi-wing, open cockpit, single-engined Steerman trainers, an antique-type plane. We wore sheepskin jackets, helmets, and goggles, and, of course, the white silk scarf.

One day a plane crashed, and one of our classmates lost his life. Flight schedules were immediately intensified. This was war; it was no time to let student pilots become jittery.

The cadets in our class had all soloed, and that afternoon found us practicing landings at an auxiliary field. At the close of the day the last in turn to use the planes were to fly them back to the main field, while the remaining cadets were transported there by bus. It was my assignment to take one of the planes across the valley to the main field.

Out of curiosity I decided to fly over the crash site. It was plainly visible from the air. One could see the spot where the plane had hit, burst into flames, and skidded across the desert floor, burning the chaparral in a long, sooty smear. My curiosity satisfied, I then headed for the base.

We had been taught the various maneuvers: stalls, loops, spins, chandelles. In order to lose altitude to enter the flight pattern I decided to put the plane into a practice spin—the quickest way, of course, to lose altitude. I followed the proper procedure, and the plane entered a normal spin.

Somehow in making the recovery from the spin (perhaps nervous at the thoughts of the accident) I was clumsy, and I overcorrected. Instead of making a recovery the plane shuddered violently, stalled, and then flipped over into a secondary spin.

Never have I known such panic—before or since. I found myself clawing at the controls. Finally the plane pulled out in a long, sweeping skid just feet above the desert floor.

I don't know what happened. I think probably I let go of the controls. The plane, although antique, was used heavily as a trainer because it had the capacity almost to fly itself if left alone.

I quickly recovered my composure and made a normal landing, hoping that no one had seen the circus performance.

When we have had a frightening experience, shock

sometimes doesn't set in until we have retired. For a long time that night I tossed and fretted, experiencing almost the same panic as I had in the plane. My buddy, a member of the Church from Salina, Utah, was sleeping in the lower bunk and was awakened in the wee hours of the morning by my restlessness. We went out on the barracks steps and talked. I told him what had happened and asked, "What did I do wrong?"

Then he told me that his instructor, early in their flight training, had warned them against just such a happening. He had pointed out to them the singular danger of a clumsy recovery from a spin and had taken each of his students up and demonstrated how to recover if it should happen. This training, this warning from his teacher, had insured my friend against mortal danger.

There arose in me an intense resentment for my instructor. Why hadn't *he* told *us?* Why hadn't he *warned* us? Another second or two in that spin and—well, I would not have been writing this story. His negligence as an instructor had come *that* close to costing me my life.

Great responsibility rests upon those of us who are teachers—both faculty members in the Church school system and teachers and general officers in the priesthood and auxiliary organizations of the Church. Jacob was a conscientious instructor:

> Wherefore I, Jacob, gave unto them these words as I taught them in the temple, having first obtained mine errand from the Lord.

For I, Jacob, and my brother Joseph had been consecrated priests and teachers of this people, by the hand of Nephi.

And we did magnify our office unto the Lord, taking upon us the responsibility, answering the sins of the people upon our own heads if we did not teach them the word of God with all diligence; wherefore, by laboring with our might their blood might not come upon our garments; otherwise their blood would come upon our garments, and we would not be found spotless at the last day. (Jacob 1:17–19.)

Our whole social order could self-destruct over the obsession with freedom disconnected from responsibility, where choice is imagined to be somehow independent of consequences.

11

PRAYERS AND ANSWERS

Many years ago John Burroughs, a naturalist, one summer evening was walking through a crowded park. Above the sounds of city life he heard the song of a bird.

He stopped and listened. Those with him had not heard it. He looked around. No one else had noticed it.

It bothered him that everyone should miss something so beautiful.

He took a coin from his pocket and flipped it into the air. It struck the pavement with a ring, no louder than the song of the bird. Everyone turned; they could hear that.

It is difficult to separate from all the sounds of city traffic the song of a bird. But you can hear it. You can hear it plainly if you train yourself to listen for it.

One of our sons has always been interested in radio. When he was a little fellow, his Christmas present was a very elementary radio construction set.

As he grew, and as we could afford it, and as he could earn it, he received more sophisticated equipment.

There have been many times over the years, some very recently, when I have sat with him as he talked with someone in a distant part of the world.

I could hear static and interference and catch a word or two, or sometimes several voices at once.

Yet he can understand, for he has trained himself to tune out the interference.

It is difficult to separate from the confusion of life that quiet voice of inspiraton. Unless you attune yourself, you will miss it.

Answers to prayers come in a quiet way. The scriptures describe that voice of inspiration as a still small voice.

If you really try, you can learn to respond to that voice.

In the early days of our marriage, our children came at close intervals. As parents of little children will know, in those years it is quite a novelty for them to get an uninterrupted night of sleep.

If you have a new baby and another youngster cutting teeth, or one with a fever, you can be up and down a hundred times a night. (That, of course, is an exaggeration. It's probably only twenty or thirty times.)

We finally divided our children into "his" and "hers" for night tending. She would get up for the new baby, and I would tend the one cutting teeth.

One day we came to realize that each would hear only the one to which we were assigned and would sleep very soundly through the cries of the other.

We have commented on this over the years, convinced that you can train yourself to hear what you want to hear, to see and feel what you desire, but it takes some conditioning.

There are so many of us who go through life and seldom, if ever, hear that voice of inspiration, because "the natural man receiveth not the things of the Spirit of God: for they are foolishness unto him: neither can he know them, because they are spiritually discerned" (1 Corinthians 2:14).

No one of us can survive in the world of today,
much less in what it soon will become,
without personal inspiration.
The spirit of reverence can and should be evident
in every organization in the Church
and in the life of every member.

12

GIVE TO THE NEEDY

Many years ago, my parents lived in a very modest home in the northern end of the state of Utah. One morning, my mother answered a knock at the door and was confronted there by a large, frightening-looking man, who asked her for money.

She said, "We have no money." There were in that home innumerable children, but very little money.

He pressed his demands, insisting that she give him some money, finally saying, "I am hungry; I would like to get something to eat."

"Well," she said, "if that is the case then I can help you." So she hurried to the kitchen and fixed him a lunch. And I am sure it was the most modest of provisions. She could tell as she gave him the lunch at the door that he was not pleased, but with little resistance he took the lunch and left.

She watched him as he went down the lane through the gate and started up the road. He looked back, but he did not

see her standing inside the door, and as he passed the property line, he took the lunch and threw it over the fence into
the brush.

Now, my mother is a little Danish woman, and she was
angered; she was angered at the ingratitude. In that house
there was nothing to waste, and she was angered that he was
so ungrateful.

The incident was forgotten until a week or two later;
she answered another knock at the door. There stood a tall,
raw-boned teenage boy, who asked about the same question
in essentially the same words: "We need help; we are hungry.
Could you give us some money; could you give us some
food?"

But somehow the image of the first man appeared in her
mind and she said, "No," excusing herself: "I am sorry. I am
busy; I cannot help you today. I just cannot help you." What
she meant was, "I won't. I won't. I won't be taken in again."

Well, the young man turned without protest and walked
out the gate, and she stood looking after him. It wasn't until
he passed through the gate that she noticed the wagon, the
father and mother and the other youngsters, and as the boy
swung his long legs into the wagon he looked back rather
poignantly; the father shook the reins and the wagon went
on down the road. She hesitated just long enough so that
she could not call them back.

From that experience she drew a moral by which she has
lived and which she has imparted to her children, and
though that was, I suppose, nearly fifty years ago, there has
always been just a tiny hint of pain as she recalled the inci-

dent with this moral: "Never fail to give that which you have to someone who is in need."

I stress to you young brothers and sisters in the Church your obligation to give that which you possess to any who may be in need. I recognize that admittedly your material substance is meager compared to the needs of the world, but your spiritual powers are equal to the needs of the world. I urge you to resolve with me that never so long as we live would anyone be hungry, spiritually or physically, that we could aid and assist.

The choice of life is not between fame and fortune,
nor between wealth and poverty,
but between good and evil.

13

KEEPING COVENANTS

I would like to tell the young people of an experience I had when I was a very young man and was talking with a very old man. This is the story he told me.

When he was a little boy—that would be nearly one hundred years ago—he lived in a very small community a long way from Salt Lake City. One of the men in the ward, a close relation to the President of the Church, had passed away. When the funeral was held, everyone in the ward went to the funeral, as was the custom. So this little boy went with his father and mother to the funeral. Just as the service was about to begin, to their great surprise in walked the prophet, the President of the Church. He had come a long way by train and then by buggy to attend the funeral service of his relative.

The service was similar to those of other funerals. Some kind things were said about the deceased man. He was described as a good man. Someone said that he had given flour to the widows, and he had helped those in the ward. We like to say kind things at funerals, of course.

The concluding speaker was the President of the Church. What he said was not comforting. He gave a talk that perhaps only the President of the Church could give; and he perhaps could speak in that way only because he was speaking about a relative. He confirmed that this man had been a good man and said that the good things he had done would earn him a reward; but then he said: "The fact is, he did not keep his covenants."

This man, when he was young, had gone to the temple to be married, to be sealed. Some sweet young girl had persuaded him to change his habits and become worthy, so he stopped doing some wrong things, began to pay his tithing and attend church, eventually received a temple recommend; and then the couple went to the temple and were sealed. But after a while, because the temple was a long way away and they did not return, he forgot. He began to slip back into some of his old habits. He forgot to pay his tithing. He ceased being the man he had become.

His relative, the President of the Church, knew all this, so he acknowledged that all the good he had done would earn him rewards, but he said, "The fact is, he did not keep his covenants." There were things he did that he should not have done, for he had covenanted not to do them. Similarly there were things he had covenanted to do that he had not done. So he had covenanted not to do some things and covenanted to do some things, and he had become loose and lazy on those things. He was basically a good man, maybe a good Christian as far as the world would judge it. But he had not kept his covenants, his agreements.

When you young people go to the temple to be married, you will hear about the importance of your marriage being sealed by the Holy Spirit of Promise. "I, the Lord, am bound when ye do what I say" (D&C 82:10). And if you do what He says, He cannot break those promises; you will receive what is promised. But if you do not keep your part of the covenant the promises will not be fulfilled. There cannot be justice in your receiving the reward if you have not earned it. . . .

When we prepare for the temple, we will be asked questions. One question will be about the Word of Wisdom. "Do you keep the Word of Wisdom?" Well, do you or don't you? Quite often when I am interviewing leaders, I will say, "Are you worthy of a temple recommend?" Often they will say, "Well, I feel I am." And I will say, "But are you worthy?" It does not matter how you feel. It matters whether you are worthy. Then the brother will smile and he will say, "I am worthy." "Do you keep your covenants?" "I keep my covenants." That is a commendable thing. . . .

Now, we must keep our covenants. "Are you morally clean?" "Do you pay your tithing?" "Do you sustain the authorities of the Church?" "Well, yes, everybody but Brother Somebody." No, that is not the way it works. Brother Somebody probably needs your sustaining influence more than anyone. Keep your covenants. Keep your covenants.

When you come to the temple and receive your endowment, and kneel at the altar and be sealed, you can live an ordinary life and be an ordinary soul—struggling against temptation, failing and repenting, and failing again and repenting, but always determined to keep your covenants—and that marriage ordinance will be sealed by the Holy Spirit of Promise. Then the day will come when you will receive the benediction: "Well done, thou good and faithful servant: thou hast been faithful over a few things, I will make thee ruler over many things; enter thou into the joy of thy lord" (Matthew 25:21).

*Obedience—that which God will never take by force—
He will accept when freely given. And He will then
return to you freedom that you can hardly dream of—
the freedom to be, at least a thousandfold more
than we offer Him. Strangely enough,
the key to freedom is obedience.*

14

OF CARS AND DATES

No age is quite so carefree, so restless, so potential as high school years. Notwithstanding the outward turmoils and nonconformity, these are years of quiet inner growth. These are years of silent, restless maturing. It is to our youth of high school years that I speak.

A few days ago I visited a large automobile dealership, where I looked at many new automobiles. One in particular caught my eye—a convertible, sports model, with all of the fancy equipment you could imagine. It had push-button everything, and more horsepower than a division of cavalry. . . . How I would have enjoyed a car like that when I was in high school! It occurred to me that you might be interested in owning such a car.

Do you have an imagination? Imagine with me that I am your benefactor; that I have decided to present to a typical teenager a car such as this, and you are the one who has been chosen. On the evening of the presentation I see that you are not quite financially able to run such a car, so I generously include free gas, oil, maintenance, tires, anything your car would use—all of this, and the bills would come to me.

How you will enjoy that car! Think of driving it to school tomorrow. Think of all the new friends you would suddenly acquire.

Now, your parents may be hesitant to let you use this car freely, so I will visit with them. I am sure they will be reluctant, but let us say that because of my position as one of the leaders of the Church they will consent.

Let us imagine, then, that you have your car, everything to run it, freedom to use it.

Suppose that one evening you are invited to attend a Church social. "There are just enough of you to ride in my station wagon," your teacher says. "You may leave your car home."

When they come to take you to the party, you suddenly remember your new convertible parked at the curb with the top down. You hastily go back into the house and give the keys to your father, asking that he put it in the garage, for it looks as though it might rain. Your father, of course, obediently agrees. (It is interesting how obedient parents have become these days.)

When you come home that evening you notice that your car is not at the curb. "Dear old Dad," you muse, "always willing to help out." But as the station wagon pulls into the driveway and the lights flash into the garage, you see it is empty.

You rush into the house, find your father, and ask that very urgent question.

"Oh, I loaned it to someone," he responds.

Then imagine, seriously imagine, a conversation such as this:

"Well, who was it?"

"Oh, that boy who comes by here regularly."

"What boy?"

"Oh, that boy . . . Well, I have seen him pass here several times on his bicycle."

"What is his name?"

"I'm afraid I didn't find out."

"Well, where did he take the car?"

"That really wasn't made clear."

"Well, when will he bring it back?"

"There really wasn't an agreement on that."

Then suppose that your father should say to you, with some impatience, "Now, just calm down. He rushed in here. He needed a car. You weren't using it. He seemed to be in a frantic hurry over something, and he looked like an honest boy, so I gave him the keys. Now, relax, and go to bed. Calm down."

I suppose that under the circumstances you would look at your father with that puzzled expression and wonder if some important connection in his thinking mechanism had slipped loose.

It would take a foolish father to loan such an expensive piece of equipment on an arrangement such as that. Particularly one that belonged to you.

I am sure that you have anticipated the moral of this little illustration, you of high school age. It is in these years that dating begins; this custom of two sets of parents loaning their teenagers to one another for the necessary and the important purpose of their finding their way into maturity, and eventually into marriage. Perhaps for the first time you notice, and you begin to resent, the interest of your parents in and their supervision of your activities. Dating leads to marriage. Marriage is a sacred religious covenant, and in its most exalted expression it may be an eternal covenant. Whatever preparation relates to marriage, whether it be personal or social, concerns us as members of the Church.

Now, I speak very plainly to you, my young friends. If you are old enough to date, you are old enough to know that your parents have not only the right but the sacred obligation, and they are under counsel from leaders of the Church, to concern themselves with your dating habits.

If you are mature enough to date, you are mature enough to accept without childish, juvenile argument their authority as parents to set rules of conduct for you.

No sensible father would loan your new convertible to anybody, to go anyplace, to do anything, to come back anytime. If you are old enough to date, you are old enough to see the very foolishness of parents who would loan their children on any such arrangement. Don't ask your parents to permit you—you, their most precious possession—to go out dating on such flimsy agreements.

Actually the loan of the car would not be as serious as you suppose, for should it be destroyed completely, it could be replaced. But there are some problems and some hazards with dating for which there is no such fortunate solution.

When you are old enough you ought to start dating. It is good for young men and women to learn to know and to appreciate one another. It is good for you to go to games and dances and picnics, to do all of the young things. We encourage our young people to date. We encourage you to set high standards of dating.

When are you old enough? Maturity may vary from individual to individual, but we are rather of the conviction that dating should not even begin until you are well into your teens. And then, ideal dating is on a group basis. None of this steady dancing, steady dating routine. Steady dating is courtship, and surely the beginning of courtship ought to be delayed until you are almost out of your teens.

Dating should not be premature. You should appreciate your parents if they see to that. Dating should not be without supervision, and you should appreciate parents who see to that. . . .

Be open with your parents. Communicate with them. Discuss your problems with them. Have prayer with them before a dating event.

Stay in group activities. Don't pair off. Avoid steady dating. The right time to begin a courtship is when you have emerged from your teens.

Heed the counsels from your bishop, from your priesthood and auxiliary teachers, from your seminary teacher.

15

TESTIMONY COMES FROM PERSONAL REVELATION

Although a testimony of this plan is of crucial importance to us, we must not count on winning many debates on the plan of redemption versus the prevailing theories and philosophies of men.

I learned a long time ago that spiritual knowledge is described in a different language than is secular knowledge.

On this I had a valuable experience before I was a General Authority. It affected me profoundly. I sat on a plane next to a professed atheist who ridiculed my belief in God. I bore my testimony to him: "There is a God. I *know* He lives!"

He said: "You don't *know*. Nobody *knows* that. You can't *know* it." When I would not yield, the atheist posed perhaps the ultimate challenge to testimony. "All right," he said in a sneering, condescending way, "you say you know." Then, "Tell me *how* you know."

I could not do it. I was helpless to communicate. When I used the words *spirit* and *witness,* the atheist responded, "I don't know what you are talking about." The words *prayer, discernment,* and *faith* also were meaningless to him.

"You see," he said, "you don't really know. If you did, you would be able to tell me *how you know.*"

Perhaps, I thought, I had borne my testimony to him unwisely, and I was at a loss as to what to do. Then came the experience. A thought, a revelation, came into my mind, and I said to the atheist: "Let me ask you a question. Do you know what salt tastes like?"

"Of course I do," was his reply.

"When did you taste salt last?"

"I just had dinner on the plane."

"You just think you know what salt tastes like," I said.

He insisted, "I know what salt tastes like as well as I know anything."

"If I gave you a cup of salt and a cup of sugar, could you tell the salt from the sugar if I let you taste them both?"

"Now you are getting juvenile," he said. "Of course I could tell the difference. I know what salt tastes like. I know it as well as I know anything."

"Then," I said, "assuming that I have never tasted salt, explain to me just what it tastes like."

After some thought, he ventured, "Well—I—uh, it is not sweet, and it is not sour."

"You've told me what it isn't, not what it is."

After several attempts, of course he could not do it. He

could not convey, in words alone, so ordinary an experience as tasting salt.

I bore testimony to him once again and said: "I know there is a God. You ridiculed that testimony and said that if I *did* know, I would be able to tell you exactly *how* I know. My friend, spiritually speaking, I have tasted salt. I am no more able to convey to you in words alone how this knowledge has come than you are able to tell me what salt tastes like. But I say to you again, there is a God! He lives! And just because you don't know, don't try to tell me that I don't know, for I do!"

As we parted, I heard him mutter: "I don't need your religion for a crutch. I don't need it."

That to me was a great lesson on personal revelation. From it I learned about prompting and the truth of the scripture which says, "Treasure up in your minds continually the words of life, and it shall be given you in the very hour that portion that shall be meted unto every man" (D&C 84:85).

Since then I have never been embarrassed or ashamed that I could not explain in words alone everything I know spiritually, or tell just how I received it. From such experiences we will surely suffer some humiliation, but that is good for our faith. And we have an ever-present guide. We will be tested, but we will never be left without help.

16

MAN'S DUAL NATURE

We are dual beings, a spirit son or daughter of God, alive and intelligent in the first estate, confined now to a body of flesh and bone. "The spirit and the body are the soul of man" (D&C 88:15). The spirit is eternal; the body will become so. There are languages we can speak and hear with the body. There are languages of the spirit, one being revelation. . . .

It should not be as difficult as it is to teach the reality of the spirit to some adults, especially those who "when they are learned they think they are wise" (2 Nephi 9:28). But the Lord taught that "except ye . . . become as little children, ye shall not enter into the kingdom of heaven" (Matthew 18:3; see also Luke 18:17; 3 Nephi 11:37–38).

Perhaps that is because little children learn quickly things that adults are slow to comprehend. A friend told me that his young son knew all about computers, and said, "I have no idea where he gets it." I said, "Probably from his younger brother or sister."

The computer is a good illustration of our dual nature.

Computers are made of metal, plastic, and glass, and can hold an astonishing amount of information—all the standard works, sets of encyclopedias, dictionaries, whole libraries, even illustrations. Press the keys, and you can select any part of what is stored and see it instantly on a screen. You can rearrange, add to, or subtract from what is stored in the computer, and can print on paper whatever you desire, even in full color. You then can hold in your hand tangible, absolute proof of what is inside that box of metal and glass and plastic.

However, should you take the computer completely apart or melt it down, you could find not one word, not one illustration—no tangible evidence that there were volumes, verses, or illustrations inside the computer. You could no more find words in the ashes of a computer than you could find the spirit in the ashes of a cremated human body.

Notwithstanding that the spirit is invisible and intangible, it is the very essence of reality. "Ye are the temple of God, and . . . the Spirit of God dwelleth in you" (1 Corinthians 3:16).

Revelation is the process of communication to the spiritual eyes and to the spiritual ears that were ours before our mortal birth. The scriptures speak of "the eyes of our understanding" (see Jeremiah 5:21; Ephesians 1:18; 2 Nephi 21:3; D&C 110:1; 138:11, 29), and of "blindness of mind" (Ether 4:15) and of heart (Deuteronomy 28:28; Ephesians 4:18; D&C 58:15). They speak of "feeling" words, rather than hearing them (1 Nephi 17:45), and of the still, small voice (1 Kings 19:12; 1 Nephi 17:45).

17

BEWARE OF
COVENANT BREAKERS

Occasionally one inside the Church joins the ranks of the critics. Beware of covenant breakers. It is one thing for non-members to criticize and attack the Church and its leaders. It is quite another when someone within the Church does so, after he has entered into solemn and sacred covenants to do otherwise. It makes a very big difference indeed.

On one occasion I attended a meeting at Ricks College with a group of seminary teachers when President Joseph Fielding Smith, then the President of the Council of the Twelve, met with us. One of the teachers asked about a letter being circulated throughout the Church at that time from a dissident member who claimed that many of the ordinances were not valid because of some supposed mistake in the procedure in conferring the priesthood. When President Smith was asked what he thought about the man's claim, he said, "Before we consider the claim, let me tell you about that man." He then told us of several things about him and about the covenants he had not kept. He concluded with this statement: "And so you see, that man is a liar, pure and simple—well, perhaps not so pure."

There are those both outside the Church and in it who will try to persuade or compel us to change our direction. The keeping of covenants is a measure of those outside of the Church as well.

An individual seeking to hold high public office, perhaps in business or in government, may claim to be worthy of trust and insist he would not cheat, not misrepresent, not mislead the public. Ask yourself, what does that individual do with a private trust? A good measure is to determine how he keeps covenants relating to his family. While one could not excuse it, one perhaps could understand that it would be somewhat easier to steal from, cheat on, or lie to an anonymous stranger, or to the public, than it would be to one's own family. Those who are not faithful to their marriage partners and to their families are hardly worthy of confidence and trust in education, in business, in government. If they would cheat on marriage vows, counting perhaps on forgiveness and tolerance that may have been extended at times, surely they must stand unworthy of any great public trust.

Beware of covenant breakers, inside the Church and out. Beware of those who mock the prophets.

In Civil War days a performer named Blondin astonished the country by crossing the Niagara River on a tightrope. On one occasion President Abraham Lincoln faced a delegation of critics and said:

Gentlemen, suppose all the property you possessed were in gold, and you had placed it in the hands of a Blondin to carry across the Niagara River on a rope. With slow, cautious steps he walks the rope, bearing your all. Would you shake the cable and keep shouting at him, "Blondin, stand up a little straighter; Blondin, stoop a little more; go a little faster; lean more to the South; now lean a little more to the North?" Would that be your behavior in such an emergency? No, you would hold your breath, every one of you, as well as your tongues. You would keep your hands off until he was safe on the other side.

This government, gentlemen, is carrying an immense weight. Untold treasures are in its hands. The persons managing the ship of state in this storm are doing the best they can. Don't worry them with needless warnings and complaints. Keep silence; be patient, and we will get you safe across. (John Wesley Hill, *Abraham Lincoln: Man of God* [New York: G. P. Putnam's Sons], p. 402.)

Keep your spiritual premiums paid up. Do not let your spiritual policy lapse. Do not cause it to be cancelled in some moment of rebellion. Extend your policy by adding endorsements as you receive the higher ordinances. Work to qualify for each of them.

I was always impressed when President Joseph Fielding Smith was asked to pray. Invariably, he would make reference to the principles and ordinances of the gospel and would always include this expression: "May we remain faithful to our covenants and obligations."

And that is my message, simply this: Be faithful to the covenants and ordinances of the gospel. Qualify for those sacred ordinances step by step. Honor the covenants connected with them, and you will be happy.

There is a position of truth—strong, powerful, steady. Somebody has to stand, face the storm, declare the truth, let the winds blow, and be serene, composed, and steady in the doing of it. Who are we anyway? Are we the ones who were born to be immune from persecution or from any penalties in connection with living and preaching the gospel?

18

"FEED MY SHEEP"

I want to talk to my young friends of the Aaronic Priesthood. I begin with a parable; and then I have a test for you.

Imagine that our bishop has appointed you and me to plan a picnic for all of the ward members. It is to be the finest social in the history of the ward, and we are to spare no expense.

We reserve a beautiful picnic ground in the country. We are to have it all to ourselves; no outsiders will interfere with us.

The arrangements go very well, and when the day comes the weather is perfect. All is beautifully ready. The tables are in one long row. We even have tablecloths and china. You have never seen such a feast. The Relief Society and the Young Women have outdone themselves. The tables are laden with every kind of delicious food: cantaloupe, watermelon, corn on the cob, fried chicken, hamburgers, cakes, pies—you get the picture.

We are seated, and the bishop calls upon the patriarch to bless the food. Every hungry youngster secretly hopes it will be a short prayer.

Then, just at that moment, there is an interruption. A noisy old car jerks into the picnic grounds and sputters to a stop close to us. We are upset. Didn't they see the Reserved signs?

A worried-looking man lifts the hood; a spout of steam comes out. One of our brethren, a mechanic, says, "That car isn't going anywhere until it is repaired."

Several children spill from the car. They are ragged and dirty and noisy. And then an anxious mother takes a box to that extra table nearby. It is mealtime. The children are hungry. She puts a few leftovers on the table. Then she nervously moves them about, trying to make it look like a meal for her hungry brood. But there is not enough.

We wait impatiently for them to quiet down so that we can have the blessing and enjoy our feast.

Then one of their little girls spies our table. She pulls her runny-nosed little brother over to us and pushes her head between you and me. We cringe aside, because they are very dirty. Then the little girl says, "Ummm, look at that. Ummm, ummm, I wonder what that tastes like."

Everyone is waiting. Why did they arrive just at that moment? Such an inconvenient time. Why must we interrupt what we are doing to bother with outsiders? Why couldn't they have stopped somewhere else? They are not clean! They are not like us. They just don't fit in.

Since the bishop has put us in charge, he expects us to handle these intruders. What should we do? Of course, this is only a parable. But now for the test. If it really happened, my young friends, what *would* you do?

I will give you three choices.

First, you could insist that the intruders keep their children quiet while we have the blessing. Thereafter we ignore them. After all, we reserved the place.

I doubt that you would do that. Could you choke down a feast before hungry children? Surely we are better than that! That is not the answer.

The next choice. There is that extra table. And we do have too much of some things. We could take a little of this and a little of that and lure the little children back to their own table. Then we could enjoy our feast without interruption. After all, we earned what we have. Did we not "obtain it by [our own] industry," as the Book of Mormon says? (See Alma 4:6.)

I hope you would not do that. There is a better answer. You already know what it is.

We should go out to them and invite them to come and join us. You could slide that way, and I could slide this way, and the little girl could sit between us. They could all fit in somewhere to share our feast. Afterwards, we will fix their car and provide something for their journey.

Could there be more pure enjoyment than seeing how much we could get those hungry children to eat? Could there be more satisfaction than to interrupt our festivities to help our mechanic fix their car?

Is that what you would do? Surely it is what you *should* do. But forgive me if I have a little doubt. Let me explain.

We, as members of the Church, have the fulness of the gospel. Every conceivable kind of spiritual nourishment is ours. Every part of the spiritual menu is included. It provides an unending supply of spiritual strength. Like the widow's cruse of oil, it is replenished as we use it and shall never fail (see 1 Kings 17:8–16).

And yet there are some people across the world and about us—our neighbors, our friends, some in our own families—who, spiritually speaking, are undernourished. Some of them are starving to death!

If we keep all our spiritual blessings to ourselves, it is not unlike feasting before those who are hungry.

We are to go out to them, and to invite them to join us. We are to be missionaries.

It does not matter if that interrupts your schooling or delays your career or your marriage—or basketball. Except those who have a serious health problem, every Latter-day Saint young man should answer the call to serve a mission. . . .

Almost any returned missionary will have a question: "If they are starving spiritually, why do they not accept what we have? Why do they slam the door on us and turn us away?" . . .

Be patient if some will not eat when first invited. Remember, not all who are spiritually hungry will accept the gospel. Do you remember how reluctant you are to try any new food? . . .

But feed them we must. We are commanded to preach the gospel to every nation, kindred, tongue, and people. That message, my young friends, appears more than eighty times in the scriptures.

I did not serve a regular mission until my wife and I were called to preside in New England. When I was of missionary age, when I was your age, young men could not be called to the mission field. It was World War II, and I spent four years in the military. But I did do missionary work; we did share the gospel. It was my privilege to baptize one of the first two Japanese to join the Church since the mission had been closed twenty-two years earlier. Brother Elliot Richards baptized Tatsui Sato. I baptized his wife, Chio. And the work in Japan was reopened. We baptized them in a swimming pool amid the rubble of a university that had been destroyed by bombs.

Shortly thereafter I boarded a train in Osaka for Yokohama and a ship that would take me home. Brother and Sister Sato came to the station to say good-bye. Many tears were shed as we bade one another farewell.

It was a very chilly night. The railroad station, what there was left of it, was very cold. Starving children were sleeping in the corners. That was a common sight in Japan in those days. The fortunate ones had a newspaper or a few old rags to fend off the cold.

On that train I slept restlessly. The berths were too short anyway. In the bleak, chilly hours of the dawn, the train stopped at a station along the way. I heard a tapping on the window and raised the blind. There on the platform stood a little boy tapping on the window with a tin can. I knew he was one of the orphans and a beggar; the tin can was the symbol of their suffering. Sometimes they carried a spoon as well, as if to say, "I am hungry; feed me."

He might have been six or seven years old. His little body was thin with starvation. He had on a thin, ragged shirt-like kimono, nothing else. His head was shingled with scabs. One side of his jaw was swollen—perhaps from an abscessed tooth. Around his head he had tied a filthy rag with a knot on top of his head—a pathetic gesture of treatment.

When I saw him and he saw that I was awake, he waved his can. He was begging. In pity, I thought, "How can I help him?" Then I remembered. I had money, Japanese money. I quickly groped for my clothing and found some yen notes in my pocket. I tried to open the window, but it was stuck. I slipped on my trousers and hurried to the end of the car. He stood outside expectantly. As I pushed at the resistant door, the train pulled away from the station. Through the dirty windows I could see him, holding that rusty tin can, with the dirty rag around his swollen jaw.

There I stood, an officer from a conquering army, heading home to a family and a future. There I stood, half-dressed, clutching some money which he had seen but which I could not get to him. I wanted to help him, but couldn't. The only comfort I draw is that I did want to help him.

That was thirty-eight years ago, but I can see him as clearly as if it were yesterday. . . .

Young brethren, I can hear the voice of the Lord saying to each of us just as He said to Peter, "Feed my lambs. . . . Feed my sheep. . . . Feed my sheep." (See John 21:15–17.)

I have unbounded confidence and faith in you, our young brethren. You are the warriors of the Restoration. And in this spiritual battle you are to relieve the spiritual hunger and feed the sheep. It is your duty!

We have the fulness of the everlasting gospel. We have the obligation to share it with those who do not have it.

The Lord provides ways to pay our debts to Him.
In one sense, we ourselves may participate in an atonement.
When we are willing to restore to others that which we
have not taken, or heal wounds that we did not inflict,
or pay a debt that we did not incur,
we are emulating His part in the Atonement.

19

STAY IN CONTEXT

Near the end of the course work for my doctorate at Brigham Young University I was enrolled with three others in a philosophy class. Two of us were completing our doctorates; the other two were just beginning their graduate work.

There arose an issue between myself and the other doctoral candidate. The professor deftly moderated the contest without taking either side. The debate became more intense, and the other two students took sides, one on each.

So there we were, two contestants, each with a "second." The issue grew more important, and each day I left the class feeling a greater failure. Why should this concern me? It concerned me because I was *right* and he was wrong, and I knew it and thought he knew it, and yet he was able to best me in every discussion. Each day I felt more inadequate, more foolish, and more tempted to capitulate.

Then one of the most important experiences of my entire education occurred. One day as we were leaving class, his "second" made the comment to me, "You're losing, aren't you?"

There was no pride left to prevent me from consenting to the obvious. "Yes, I'm losing."

"Do you know what's the matter with you?" he asked.

I became interested and answered, "I would like very much to know."

"The trouble with you," he said, "is that you are fighting out of context."

I asked him what he meant; I didn't know and he couldn't explain it. He just said, "You are fighting out of context."

That night I thought continuously about it. It wasn't the grade or the credit I was concerned about—it was bigger than that. I was being beaten and humiliated in my efforts to defend a principle that was true. The statement, "You are fighting out of context" stayed in my mind. Finally, in my humiliation I went before the Lord in prayer. Then I knew.

The next day we returned to class, this time to stay in context. When the debate was renewed, instead of mumbling some stilted, sophisticated, philosophical statement, calculated to show I was conversant with philosophical terminology and had read a book or two, instead of saying, "The a priori acquisition of intelligence as though from some external source of enlightenment," I stayed in context and said, "Revelation from God."

Suddenly the tables were turned. I was rescued from defeat, and I learned a lesson I would not forget. I stand in debt to the unassuming student from whose remark I learned so much.

All of us need to learn, seek, grow. If you are a student, go on for advanced degrees, rise to prominence in your chosen field. In any event, you needn't be unwise or immature by seeking to impose your religious convictions on others. But, when discussing the Church or the gospel, don't be drawn out of context.

Certainly you will not be able to persuade everyone to accept your views. Be wise enough to know when not to try. You can, however, inform people clearly enough that, accept them or not, they know what your convictions are. In this way, teach faith, repentance, baptism. . . .

In any field of knowledge, there are prerequisites. At a university, for example, a number of courses there are required prerequisites. You cannot register for Chemistry 371 without first having taken Chemistry 106. To enroll in Education 657 you must first have completed either Education 460 or 550. And so on. If you take the advanced course first without the prerequisite or equivalent training, likely you will founder. Without knowledge of the basic principles of a discipline, you may misunderstand, even reject, elements that are positively true when related to foundation principles of the discipline.

In the gospel there are some prerequisite courses without which the deeper meaning of some principles of the gospel may not be understood, in fact which may be completely misunderstood. For instance, the conditions under which personal revelation can be received could hardly be accepted or understood by one who has not completed the prerequisite courses of faith, repentance, baptism, and the reception of the Holy Ghost.

The bottom line is that we must never allow ourselves to be ashamed of the gospel because someone doesn't agree with us, even if that person is apparently alert, intelligent, and well-intentioned. Don't falter because you can't explain it in his terminology, in his context.

Recognize, too, that there must needs be opposition, that you cannot be totally faithful to the gospel yet popular with everybody. In fact, you can't be *anything* and be fully accepted by everybody!

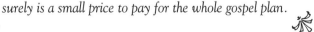

*N*o other dispensation has had the gospel without any challenge, without any opposition or resistance, without persecution from the world, and to expect that we shall be without such conditions is to expect that which will never be. We do not hold membership in the Church and its blessings without paying a price for it.
But a scoffing, cynical remark or a scornful glance surely is a small price to pay for the whole gospel plan.

20

FORGIVING ONESELF

Sometimes, even after confession and penalties, the most difficult part of repentance is to forgive oneself. President Joseph Fielding Smith told of a woman who had repented of immoral conduct and was struggling to find her way. She asked him what she should do now. In turn, he asked her to read to him from the Old Testament the account of Sodom and Gomorrah, of Lot, and of Lot's wife, who was turned to a pillar of salt (see Genesis 19:26). Then he asked her what lesson those verses held for her.

She answered, "The Lord will destroy those who are wicked."

"Not so," President Smith told this repentant woman. "The lesson for *you* is *'Don't look back!'*"

21

CHANNELING AND CONTROLLING YOUR THOUGHTS

When I was about ten years old, we lived in a home surrounded by an orchard. There never seemed to be enough water for the trees. The ditches were always fresh-plowed in the spring, but after the first few irrigating turns, the weeds would spring up in the ditch bottoms and soon they were choked with water grass, June grass, and redroot. One day, in charge of the irrigating turn, I found myself in trouble. As the water moved down the rows choked with weeds, it carried enough leaves and grass and debris to lodge against the weed stocks and flood the water from the ditch. I raced through the puddles, trying to build the banks up a little higher, to keep the water in the channel. As soon as I had one break patched up there would be another one flooding over in another spot.

About that time an older brother came through the lot with a friend of his who was majoring in agriculture. He watched me for a moment, then with a few vigorous strokes of the shovel he cleared the weeds from the dampened ditch bottom and allowed the water to course through the channel he had dug.

"You will waste the whole irrigating turn patching up the banks," he said. "If you want the water to stay on its course, you have to make a place for it to go."

I have learned that thoughts, like water, will follow the course if we *make* a place for them to go. Otherwise, we may spend all our time frantically patching up the banks and may find that our "turn" is over and that we have wasted the day of our probation. . . .

I want to tell you of one way you can control your thoughts. It is simple. It may seem so elementary that you will think it unimportant. But, if you will, it may help you.

The mind is like a stage. Except when we are asleep, the curtain is always up. Always there is some act being performed on that stage. It may be a laughing comedy or an aggrieved and tragic drama. It may be interesting or dull. It may be clear or it may be confused. It may be strenuous or perhaps relaxing. But *always*, except when we are asleep, *always* there is some act playing on that stage of the mind.

Have you noticed that, without any real intent on your part and almost in the midst of any performance, a shady little thought may creep in from the wings and endeavor to attract your attention? These delinquent little thoughts, these unsavory characters, will try to upstage everybody. If you permit them to go on, all other thoughts, of any virtue, will leave the stage. You will be left, because you consented to it, to the influence of unworthy thoughts.

If you pay attention to them, if you yield to them, they will enact for you on this stage of the mind, anything to the limit of your toleration. It may be vulgar, immoral, depraved, ugly. Their theme may be of bitterness, jealousy, excessive grief, even hatred. When they have the stage, if you let them, they will devise the cleverest persuasions to hold your attention. They can make it interesting, all right, even apparently innocent—for they are but thoughts.

What do you do at a time like this, when the stage of your mind is commandeered by these imps of unclean thinking? Whether they be the gray ones that look almost white; or the dustier ones, more questionable yet; or the filthy ones, which leave no room for doubt, what do you do?

This, then, is what I would teach you: Let me suggest that you choose from among the sacred music of the Church one favorite hymn. I have reason for suggesting that it be a Latter-day Saint hymn, one with lyrics that are uplifting and the music reverent. Select one that, when it is properly rendered, makes you feel something akin to inspiration.

Now, go over it in your mind very thoughtfully a few times. Memorize the words and the music. Even though you have had no musical training, even though you do not play an instrument, and even though your voice may leave something to be desired, you can think through a hymn. I suspect you already have a favorite. I have stressed how important it is to know that you can only think of *one* thing at a time. Use this hymn as your emergency channel. Use this as the place for your thoughts to go. Anytime you find that these shady actors have slipped in from the sideline of your thinking onto the stage of your mind, think through this hymn. "Put the record on," as it were, and then you will begin to know something about controlling your thoughts. "Music is one of the most forceful instruments for governing the mind and spirit of man" (William F. Gladstone). It will change the whole mood on the stage of your mind. Because it is clean and uplifting and reverent, the baser thoughts will leave.

While virtue, by choice, *will not* endure the presence of filth, that which is debased and unclean *cannot* endure the light.

Virtue *will not* associate with filth, while evil *cannot* tolerate the presence of good. . . .

At first this simple little procedure may seem to you so trivial as to be unimportant and ineffective. With a little experimenting, you will learn that it is not easy, but it is *powerfully* effective.

22

SPIRITUAL CROCODILES

I always wanted to go to Africa and see the animals, and finally that opportunity came. Sister Packer and I were assigned to tour the South Africa Mission with President and Sister Howard Badger. We had a very strenuous schedule and had dedicated eight chapels in seven days, scattered across that broad continent.

President Badger was vague about the schedule for September 10. (That happens to be my birthday.) We were in Rhodesia, planning, I thought, to return to Johannesburg, South Africa. But he had other plans, and we landed at Victoria Falls.

"There is a game reserve some distance from here," he explained, "and I have rented a car, and tomorrow, your birthday, we are going to spend seeing the African animals." . . .

I talked with a young ranger, and he was surprised that I knew many of the African birds. Then he volunteered to [host us for a while]. . . .

On the way to the lookout he volunteered to show us some lions. He turned off through the brush and before long located a group of seventeen lions all sprawled out asleep and drove right up among them.

We stopped at a water hole to watch the animals come to drink. It was very dry that season and there was not much water, really just muddy spots. When the elephants stepped into the soft mud the water would seep into the depression and the animals would drink from the elephant tracks.

The antelope, particularly, were very nervous. They would approach the mud hole, only to turn and run away in great fright. I could see there were no lions about and asked the guide why they didn't drink. His answer, and this is the lesson, was "crocodiles."

I knew he must be joking and asked him seriously, "What is the problem?" The answer again: "Crocodiles."

"Nonsense," I said. "There are no crocodiles out there. Anyone can see that."

I thought he was having some fun at the expense of his foreign game expert, and finally I asked him to tell us the truth. Now, I remind you that I was not uninformed. I had read many books. Besides, anyone would know that you can't hide a crocodile in an elephant track.

He could tell I did not believe him and determined, I suppose, to teach me a lesson. We drove to another location where the car was on an embankment above the muddy hole where we could look down. "There," he said. "See for yourself."

I couldn't see anything except the mud, a little water, and the nervous animals in the distance. Then all at once I saw it—a large crocodile, settled in the mud, waiting for some unsuspecting animal to get thirsty enough to come for a drink.

Suddenly I became a believer. When he could see I was willing to listen, he continued with the lesson. "There are crocodiles all over the park," he said, "not just in the rivers. We don't have any water without a crocodile somewhere near it, and you'd better count on it."

The guide was kinder to me than I deserved. My know-it-all challenge to his first statement, "crocodiles," might have brought an invitation, "Well, go out and see for yourself!"

I could see for myself that there were no crocodiles. I was so sure of myself I think I might have walked out just to see what was there. Such an arrogant approach could have been fatal! But he was patient enough to teach me.

My young friends, I hope you'll be wiser in talking to your guides than I was on that occasion. That smart-aleck idea that I knew everything really wasn't worthy of me, nor is it worthy of you. I'm not very proud of it, and I think I'd be ashamed to tell you about it except that telling you may help you. . . .

On another trip to Africa I discussed this experience with a game ranger in another park. He assured me that you can *indeed* hide a crocodile in an elephant track—one big enough to bite a man in two.

He then showed me a place where a tragedy had occurred. A young man from England was working in the hotel for the season. In spite of constant and repeated warnings, he went through the compound fence to check something across a shallow splash of water that didn't cover his tennis shoes.

"He wasn't two steps in," the ranger said, "before a crocodile had him, and we could do nothing to save him."

It seems almost to be against our natures, particularly when we are young, to accept much guidance from others. But, young people, there are times when, regardless of how much we think we know or how much we think we want to do something, our very existence depends on paying attention to the guides.

Now, it is a gruesome thing to think about that young man who was eaten by the crocodile. But that is not, by any means, the worst thing that could happen. There are moral and spiritual things far worse even than the thought of being chewed to pieces by a monstrous lizard.

Fortunately, there are guides enough in life to prevent these things from happening if we are willing to take counsel now and again.

Some of us are appointed now, as you will be soon, to be guides and rangers. Now, we don't use those titles very much. We go under the titles of parents—father and mother—bishop, leader, adviser. Our assignment is to see that you get through mortality without being injured by these spiritual crocodiles. . . .

If you will listen to the counsel of your parents and your teachers and your leaders when you are young, you can learn how to follow the best guide of all—the whisperings of the Holy Spirit. That is individual revelation. There is a process through which we can be alerted to spiritual dangers. Just as surely as that guide warned me, you can receive signals alerting you to the spiritual crocodiles that lurk ahead.

The gospel is good medicine.
Study it and there emerges just the right
combination of direction, inspiration, caution,
admonition, understanding, and assurance
to steady and strengthen and heal.
That is a testimony that the gospel is
full and whole and true.

23

SOMEONE TO DO FOR

Shortly after the funeral held for the first wife of President Harold B. Lee, I was in a group which included his daughter Helen. Someone expressed sympathy to her for the passing of her mother and said: "She took such good care of your father. I'm sure he must be lonely and must miss all of the things she did for him."

Helen responded with an insight of remarkable wisdom. "You do not understand," she said. "It is not so much that he misses all of the things that Mother did for him. He misses her most because he needs *somebody to do for*."

We all need *someone to do for*. When that is unfulfilled as a need, we become lonely. In the Lord's own way, Relief Society provides for that need.

24

WHAT DO YOU PUT INTO IT?

Recently I listened to several sisters discuss Relief Society. One young woman said: "We find it so difficult to interest both the older and the younger women. If we have a lesson or project the younger women are interested in, the older women do not come. It's so hard to get something to please everyone."

Sisters, to me there is something pathetic about those of our sisters who sit at home waiting to be enticed to Relief Society. That is not right!

When faithful sisters pray and work and make a worthy presentation, they deserve your support. Just to have you attend is a great help.

Some sisters, it appears, seem to pore over the offering of Relief Society like a fussy diner searching a menu for something to excite the taste.

Sisters, it is your duty to attend Relief Society, just as it is the duty of the brethren to attend their priesthood meetings.

I've heard some sisters say, "I don't attend Relief Society because I just don't get anything out of it."

Let me teach you a lesson.

In 1888 the Relief Society and the young women's organizations of the Church became charter members of the National Council of Women and of the International Council. These two organizations were established primarily to promote women's suffrage and to improve the lot of women and children everywhere.

During those years our delegates had their good days and their bad, depending upon circumstances, the leadership, and the leaders' attitude toward the Mormons.

In April of 1945 Belle Smith Spafford became the general president of the Relief Society. Only a week or two after she had been sustained a letter came from the National Council of Women announcing their annual meeting to be held in New York City.

Sister Spafford had attended those meetings before, and in view of her previous experience she and her counselors carefully considered the invitation for several weeks. They decided to recommend to the President of the Church that the Relief Society terminate its membership in those councils. They prepared a statement of recommendation, listing all of the reasons for so doing.

Trembling and uncertain, Sister Spafford placed the paper on the desk of President George Albert Smith, saying, "The Relief Society Presidency wishes to recommend that the general board terminate its membership in the National

Council and in the International Council of Women, for the reasons listed on this paper."

President Smith carefully read the paper. Had they not held membership for well over half a century? he inquired.

Sister Spafford explained how costly it was to go to New York, the time it took, and described the humiliation they occasionally experienced. She recommended that they withdraw because "we don't get a thing from these councils."

This wise old prophet tipped back in his chair and looked at her with a disturbed expression. "You want to withdraw because you don't get anything out of it?" he questioned.

"That is our feeling," she replied.

"Tell me," he said, "what is it that you are putting into it?"

"Sister Spafford," he continued, "you surprise me. Do you always think in terms of what you get? Don't you think also in terms of what you have to give?"

He returned that paper to her and extended his hand. With considerable firmness he said, "You continue your membership in these councils and make your influence felt."

And so they did! Sister Spafford took the gentle correction from that wise prophet, and the day came that she was president of that organization.

Now, I pass that same message to each sister in the Church. If you are absenting yourself from Relief Society because "you don't get anything out of it," tell me, dear sister, what is it that you are putting into it?

25

PREMORTAL LIFE

Essential facts about our premortal life have been revealed. Although they are sketchy, they unravel the mystery of life.

When we comprehend the doctrine of premortal life, we know that we are the children of God, that we lived with Him in spirit form before entering mortality. We know that this life is a test, that life did not begin with birth, nor will it end with death. Then life begins to make sense, with meaning and purpose even in all of the chaotic mischief that mankind creates for itself.

Imagine that you are attending a football game. The teams seem evenly matched. One team has been trained to follow the rules. The other, to do just the opposite; they are committed to cheat and disobey every rule of sportsmanlike conduct.

While the game ends in a tie, it is determined that it must continue until one side wins decisively.

Soon the field is a quagmire. Players on both sides are being ground into the mud. The cheating of the opposing team turns to brutality. Players are carried off the field. Some have been injured critically; others, it is whispered, fatally. It ceases to be a game and becomes a battle.

You become very frustrated and upset. "Why let this go on? Neither team can win. It must be stopped."

Imagine that you confront the sponsor of the game and demand that he stop this useless, futile battle. You say it is senseless and without purpose. Has he no regard at all for the players?

He calmly replies that he will not call the game. You are mistaken. There is a great purpose in it. You have not understood.

He tells you that this is not a spectator sport—it is for the participants. It is for their sake that he permits the game to continue. Great benefit may come to them because of the challenges they face.

He points to players sitting on the bench, suited up, eager to enter the game. "When each one of them has been in, when each has met the day for which he has prepared so long and trained so hard, then, and only then, will I call the game."

Until then it may not matter which team seems to be ahead. The present score is really not crucial. There are games within games, you know. Whatever is happening to the team, each player will have his day.

Those players on the team that keep the rules will not

be eternally disadvantaged by the appearance that their team somehow always seems to be losing.

In the field of destiny, no team or player will be eternally disadvantaged because they keep the rules. They may be cornered or misused, even defeated for a time. But individual players on that team, regardless of what appears on the scoreboard, may already be victorious.

Each player will have a test sufficient to his needs; how each responds is the test.

When the game is finally over, you and they will see purpose in it all, may even express gratitude for having been on the field during the darkest part of the contest.

I do not think the Lord is quite so hopeless about what's going on in the world as we are. He could put a stop to all of it at any moment. But He will not! Not until every player has a chance to meet the test for which we were preparing before the world was, before we came into mortality.

The same testing in troubled times can have quite opposite effects on individuals. Three verses from the Book of Mormon, which is another testament of Christ, teach us that

they had had wars, and bloodsheds, and famine, and affliction, for the space of many years.

And there had been murders, and contentions, and dissensions, and all manner of iniquity among the people of Nephi; nevertheless for the righteous' sake, yea, because of the prayers of the righteous, they were spared.

But behold, because of the exceedingly great length of the war between the Nephites and the Lamanites many had become *hardened,* because of the exceedingly great length of the war; and many were softened because of their afflictions, insomuch that they did humble themselves before God, even in the depth of humility. (Alma 62:39–41, emphasis added.)

Surely you know some whose lives have been filled with adversity who have been mellowed and strengthened and refined by it, while others have come away from the same test bitter and blistered and unhappy.

We live in a day when the adversary stresses on every hand the philosophy of instant gratification. We seem to demand instant everything, including instant solutions to our problems. . . . It was meant to be that life would be a challenge. To suffer some anxiety, some depression, some disappointment, even some failure is normal.

26

THE INHERITANCE—
A PARABLE

Once a man received as his inheritance two keys. The first key, he was told, would open a vault which he must protect at all cost. The second key was to a safe within the vault which contained a priceless treasure. He was to open this safe and freely use the precious things which were stored therein. He was warned that many would seek to rob him of his inheritance. He was promised that if he used the treasure worthily it would be replenished and never be diminished, not in all eternity. He would be tested. If he used it to benefit others, his own blessings and joy would increase.

The man went alone to the vault. His first key opened the door. He tried to obtain the treasure with the other key, but he could not, for there were two locks on the safe. His key alone would not open it. No matter how he tried, he could not open it. He was puzzled. He had been given the keys. He knew the treasure was rightfully his. He had obeyed instructions, but he could not open the safe.

In due time, a woman came into the vault. She too held a key. It was noticeably different from the key he held. Her key fit the other lock. It humbled him to learn that he could not obtain his rightful inheritance without her.

They made a covenant that together they would open the treasure and, as instructed, he would watch over the vault and protect it; she would watch over the treasure. She was not concerned that, as guardian of the vault, he held two keys, for his full purpose was to see that she was safe as she watched over that which was most precious to them both. Together they opened the safe and partook of their inheritance. They rejoiced, for, as promised, it replenished itself.

With great joy they found that they could pass the treasure on to their children; each could receive a full measure, undiminished to the last generation.

Perhaps some few of their posterity would not find a companion who possessed the complementary key, or one worthy and willing to keep the covenants relating to the treasure. Nevertheless, if they kept the commandments, they would not be denied even the smallest blessing.

Because some tempted them to misuse their treasure, they were careful to teach their children about keys and covenants.

There came, in due time, among their posterity some few who were deceived or jealous or selfish because one was given two keys and another only one. The selfish ones reasoned, "Why cannot the treasure be mine alone to use as I desire?"

Some tried to reshape the key they had been given to resemble the other key. Perhaps, they thought, it would then fit both locks. And so it was that the safe was closed to them. Their reshaped keys were useless, and their inheritance was lost.

On the other hand those who received the treasure with gratitude and obeyed the laws concerning it knew joy without bounds through time and all eternity.

*You need not be either rich or hold high position
to be completely successful and truly happy.
In fact, if these things come to you, and they may,
true success must be achieved in spite of them,
not because of them.*

INDEX

— A —

Activity, Church, 24–30
Administrations. *See* Bless-
    ings
Adversary. *See* Satan
Adversity, 59, 65, 91–94
Africa, 82–86
Agency, 41, 47
Airplane (story), 38–40,
    57–59
Alma, on testimony, 25
Anger, 46
Atheist (story), 57–59
Atonement, 72
Automobiles, accidents in,
    24–25
    and dating, 52–56

— B —

Badger, Howard, 82
Balm of Gilead, 14–19
Beggars, 45–47, 70–71

Bitterness, 14–18
Blessings, 27–28
Blondin (performer), 63–64
Boy, lost (story), 4–6
Brigham City, Utah, 1
Brigham Young University,
    73
Building fund, 32
Burroughs, John, 42

— C —

Cars, accidents in (story),
    24–25
    and dating, 52–56
Celestial marriage. *See*
    Temple marriage
Children, 60
Choices, 8, 41, 47
Christianity, 35
Church of Jesus Christ of
    Latter-day Saints, The,
    34–37
Computer (analogy), 60–61

Confidence, 63
Consequences, 41
Context, staying in, 73–76
Corinne, Utah, 1
Courtship, 56
    See also Dating
Covenants, breaking of,
        62–65
    keeping of, 48–51
Creditors, 7–10
Criticism, 62–64
Crocodiles (story), 82–86

— D —

Dating, 52–56
Debate, philosophy (story),
        73–76
Debtors, 7–10
Devil. *See* Satan
Disappointment, 14–18
Duality, of man, 60–61

— E —

Empty lot (analogy), 14–15
Endowment (ordinance), 50
Envy, 14–18
Eternal marriage. *See* Temple
        marriage

— F —

Fast offerings, 32
Fire (story), 1–3
Food storage, 22
Football game (analogy),
        91–93
Forgiveness, 8–10, 68–69, 77
Free agency. *See* Agency
Freedom, 41
Funeral (story), 48–49, 87

— G —

Geshem, 21
Gilead, 14
Gladstone, William F., 81
Good and evil, 23, 47
Gratification, 94
Gratitude, 6
Grief, 14–18
Grudges, 14–18
Guidance, 85

— H —

Handcart pioneers, 4–6
Happiness, 30, 65
Hobbies, gospel, 37
Holy Ghost, 1–3, 37, 43, 86

Home teaching, 11–13, 25
Humiliation, 59, 74, 90
Humility, 37
Hymns, and thoughts, 80–81

— I —

Inactivity, Church, 24–30
Ingratitude, 46
Inheritance, the (parable),
    95–97
Inspiration. *See* Holy Ghost;
    Revelation
Instant gratification, 94
Intelligence, 37
International Council of
    Women, 89–90
Intruders (parable), 66–69
Irrigation ditch (story),
    78–79
Israelites, 20–23

— J —

Jacob (son of Lehi), on
    teaching, 40–41
Japan, 70–71
Jealousy, 14–18, 96
Jesus Christ, 7–10, 72
    on peace, 19

Johannesburg, South Africa,
    82
"John is Inactive . . . Why?"
    (article), 25
Jordan, 14
Junkyard (analogy), 14–15
Justice, 8–10

— K —

Keyboard (analogy), 36
Keys, two (parable), 95–97

— L —

LDS Hospital, 24
Leaders, criticism of, 63–64
Lee, Harold B., 87
Lee, Wilford B., "John is In-
    active . . . Why?", 25
Lincoln, Abraham, on criti-
    cism of leaders, 63–64
Lost boy (story), 4–6
Lost sheep (analogy), 24–30
Lot (Bible patriarch), 77

— M —

Man, nature of, 44, 60–61
Marriage, 11–13, 49–50, 55

McArthur, Brother, 4
Mediator (story), 7–10
Mercy, 8–10
Missionary work, 4–6, 31, 34,
    69–70
Mortality, 91–94
Music, and thoughts, 80–81

— N —

National Council of Women,
    89–90
Natural man, 44
Needy people, 45–47, 70–71
Nehemiah, 20–23
Neutrality, 23
New England Mission, 70

— O —

Ono, plains of, 21–22
Orphans, 71
Osaka, Japan, 70

— P —

Packer, Emma, 1–3, 45–47
Packer, Ira, 1–3
Panhandlers. *See* Beggars
Parker, Ann, 4–6

Parker, Arthur, 4–6
Parker, Robert, 4–6
Patience, 69, 84
Peace, 19
Persecution, 76
Personal revelation, 44,
    57–59, 76, 86
Philosophy class (story),
    73–76
Piano (analogy), 36
Picnic (parable), 66–69
Pioneers, 4–6
Plane. *See* Airplane (story)
Poor, the, 45–47, 70–71
Prayer, 3, 18, 21, 33, 42–44,
    64, 74
Preaching the gospel. *See*
    Missionary work
Premortal life, 91–94
Pride, 74
Priesthood, 25, 27–28, 37, 62
    meetings of the, 88

— R —

Radio (story), 42–43
Red shawl (story), 4–6
Refuge, 20–23
Relief Society, 20–23, 87,
    88–90

Repentance, 30
Revelation, 61
  personal, 44, 57–59, 76,
    86
Rhodesia, 82
Richards, Elliot, 70
Riches, 97
Ricks College (Idaho), 62
Rules, 92–93

— S —

Sacrament meeting, 26
Salina, Utah, 40
Salt Lake City, Utah, 4, 12,
    24
Salt (story), 57–59
Sanballat, 21
Sanctuary, 20–23
Satan, 94
Sato, Chio, 70
Sato, Tatsui, 70
Scottsdale, Ariz., 38
Selfishness, 96
Seminary teachers, 62–63
Service, 87
Shame, 14–18
Sharing the gospel. *See* Mis-
    sionary work
Shawl, red (story), 4–6

Sheep, feeding of, 66–72
  lost, 24–30
Smith, George Albert, 89–90
Smith, Joseph Fielding,
    62–63, 64
  "Don't look back!", 77
Sodom and Gomorrah, 77
South Africa Mission, 82
Spafford, Belle Smith, 89–90
Stage (analogy), 79–80
Standards, 31–33
Starvation, 24–25, 71

— T —

Teaching, 11–13, 38–41, 84
Teenagers, 52–56
Temple marriage, 13, 49–50
  See also Marriage
Testimony, 25–30, 57–59, 86
Thoughts, 15, 78–81
Tithing, 31–33, 49
Tobiah, 20–23
Trials. *See* Adversity
Trust, 63
Truth, 35, 65

— V —

Vacant lot (analogy), 14–15

— W —

Walters, Archer, 4, 6
War, 23
Welfare, principles, 45–47,
        70–71
    program, 32
Word of Wisdom, 50
World War II, 38–40, 70
Worry, 14–18

— Y —

Yokohama, Japan, 70
Youth, 52–56

About the Author

Boyd K. Packer, Acting President of the Quorum of the Twelve Apostles, has been a member of the Quorum since 1970 and a General Authority since 1961. Immediately prior to that he was supervisor of seminaries and institutes for the Church. He is a former president of the New England States Mission.

He was born in Brigham City, Utah. Following his graduation from high school, he served as a pilot in the U.S. Air Force during World War II. After the war he obtained his bachelor's and master's degrees, and then received his doctorate in education from Brigham Young University. He is the author of many books, including *The Things of the Soul, Teach Ye Diligently, The Holy Temple, "That All May Be Edified,"* and *Let Not Your Heart Be Troubled.*

President Packer is married to Donna Edith Smith, and the couple have ten children.

51495

ISBN 1-57008-336-3
SKU 3513746
$14.95